Digging Up the Dead

PRESERVING THE DEAD

By Ryan Nagelhout

Gareth Stevens
PUBLISHING

Please visit our website, www.garethstevens.com. For a free color catalog of all our high-quality books, call toll free 1-800-542-2595 or fax 1-877-542-2596.

Library of Congress Cataloging-in-Publication Data

Nagelhout, Ryan.
Preserving the dead / by Ryan Nagelhout.
p. cm. — (Digging up the dead)
Includes index.
ISBN 978-1-4824-1271-0 (pbk.)
ISBN 978-1-4824-1234-5 (6-pack)
ISBN 978-1-4824-1488-2 (library binding)
1. Funeral rites and ceremonies — History — Juvenile literature. 2. Burial — Juvenile literature. 3. Death — Social aspects — Juvenile literature. I. Nagelhout, Ryan. II. Title.
GT3150.N34 2015
393—d23

First Edition

Published in 2015 by
Gareth Stevens Publishing
111 East 14th Street, Suite 349
New York, NY 10003

Copyright © 2015 Gareth Stevens Publishing

Designer: Andrea Davison-Bartolotta
Editor: Greg Roza

Photo credits: Cover, p. 1 Patrick Landmann/Getty Images; cover, back cover, pp. 1–32 (background dirt texture) Kues/Shutterstock.com; pp. 4, 7, 9, 10, 13, 15, 17, 19, 21, 22, 25, 27, 28 (gravestone) jayfish/Shutterstock.com; p. 5 Ann Ronan Pictures/Print Collector/Getty Images; p. 6 Christina Gascoigne/Robert Harding World Imagery/Getty Images; p. 7 (inset) John Elk/Lonely Planet Images/Getty Images; p. 7 (main) Quadriga Images/LOOK/Getty Images; p. 8 Sven Hoppe/picture-alliance/dpa/AP Images; p. 9 (top) Paul Hanny/Gamma-Rapho via Getty Images; p. 9 (bottom) Jake Norton/Mallory & Irvine/Getty Images; p. 11 Claudio Santana/AFP/Getty Images; pp. 12–13 Danita Delimont/Gallo Images/Getty Images; p. 13 (top) Katoe Garrod/AWL Images/Getty Images; p. 15 Huangdan2060/Wikimedia Commons; p. 16 DeAgostini/Getty Images; p. 17 Roberto Vannucci/E+/Getty Images; p. 18 mountainpix/Shutterstock.com; p. 19 Vladimir Wrangel/Shutterstock.com; p. 21 Dario Mitidieri/Photonica World/Getty Images; p. 23 Frank Bienewald/Light Rocket via Getty Images; p. 24 Alan Ramsay/Wikimedia Commons; p. 25 Universal History Archive/UIG via Getty Images; p. 27 Photographee eu/Shutterstock.com; p. 29 (main) Jeff Topping/Getty Images; p. 29 (inset) Getty Images Sport/Getty Images.

Printed in the United States of America

CPSIA compliance information: Batch #CS15GS: For further information contact Gareth Stevens, New York, New York at 1-800-542-2595.

CONTENTS

Words in the glossary appear in **bold** type
the first time they are used in the text.

IT STARTS WHEN IT ENDS

What happens to your body after you die? It depends on who you are, where you're from, and what you believe. For thousands of years, people have participated in a wide variety of death **rituals**. Some cultures let dead bodies decay or allow animals to pick them clean. In the past, a few cultures even ate their dead! Many cultures honor the dead by preserving their bodies.

A body buried in a coffin can take up to 50 years to completely break down. However, people have learned how to preserve a body for much longer than that. Ancient cultures developed methods of keeping bodies from decaying for thousands of years. Modern **embalming** methods can do a variety of things to keep a body looking healthy and alive—long after someone has died.

GRAVE MATTERS

A stiffening of the muscles—called rigor mortis—starts in bodies about 3 hours after they die. *Rigor* is Latin for "stiffness," and *mortis* is Latin for "death."

Left to the elements, a human body's tissues can decay completely in about 2 weeks.

The Ticking Clock

As soon as a person dies, their body begins to **decompose**. It becomes stiff, and the cells and organs that make up a body start to break down. Water and oxygen help speed up the decaying process. Insects and other animals make a body decompose faster when they eat it. Keeping a body away from natural elements and animals, as well as working quickly, lets people preserve a body for many years.

BOG BODIES

While humans have worked hard to develop ways to keep bodies preserved, there are some natural ways in which people become **mummified**. Many ancient bodies were preserved by peat bogs in northern Europe. A bog is a wet, spongy area somewhat like a marsh or swamp.

Peat bogs are made when plants such as **sphagnum**, or peat moss, die and partly decay in water. Bogs are cold and acidic, and lack oxygen. In this **environment**, a body can't decompose, although its bones are partly broken down by the acid. Bog mummies look different from other mummies because of this—their skin looks like leather, and the bodies are usually bag-like. Bog bodies include some of the most naturally well-preserved prehistoric bodies and help scientists learn more about life in the past.

Tollund Man

One of the most famous peat-bog mummies is named Tollund Man. Discovered in 1950 in Silkeborg, Denmark, by two brothers digging for peat, he was so well preserved that people first thought he had recently been murdered. Scientists were later called in, and they discovered the body was more than 2,000 years old. Tollund Man had a rope around his neck, and scientists determined that he had been strangled to death around age 30 or 40.

More than a thousand peat-bog mummies have been discovered in Denmark alone.

GRAVE MATTERS

Scientists even know what Tollund Man's last meal was. They found gruel—a thin porridge made of plants—in his intestines.

FROZEN IN TIME

Oxygen is needed for a body to decompose. That's why extreme cold that leads to freezing can also keep bodies well preserved. Bodies found frozen in ice are particularly well preserved and let scientists learn a lot about the period during which they lived, the clothes they wore, and even what they ate.

The frozen mummy that's been named Ötzi was discovered in 1991 on the border between Austria and Italy. Ötzi lived more than 5,000 years ago, between 3350 BC and 3100 BC. He was around 45 when he died, stood 5 feet 3 inches (160 cm) tall, and weighed about 110 pounds (50 kg). By studying his genetics and body structure, scientists have learned a lot about how humans evolved over the thousands of years between his freeze and thaw.

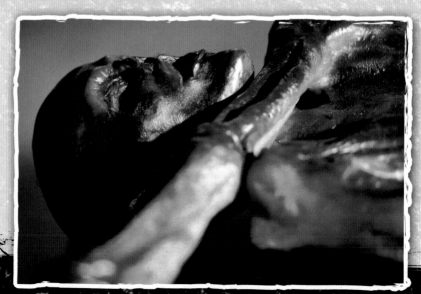

Many of the most well-preserved mummies, like Ötzi, are found by accident.

Frozen on Everest

In 1924, climber George Mallory went missing on Mount Everest in an attempt to reach the top, which is the highest point on Earth. Mallory was last spotted about 800 feet (244 m) from the summit but was never seen again. In 1999, scientists discovered his body—frozen solid. He died from a violent fall. Found exactly 75 years later, Mallory's body was perfectly preserved, with only the skin and hair bleached by the sun. His climbing partner, Andrew Irvine, has not been found.

George Mallory's body

GRAVE MATTERS

No photos of Mallory's face were taken, but the scientists said he looked just like he did in 1924.

MUD AND STICKS

Most people think of the Egyptians and their enormous limestone pyramids when it comes to mummies, but other cultures were preserving their dead thousands of years before them. The first known mummies were created by a South American tribe called the Chinchorro.

The Chinchorro were a prehistoric fishing culture that lived on the Pacific coast of modern-day Peru and Chile. For more than 3,500 years, the Chinchorro people took great pains to mummify their dead. The earliest known Chinchorro mummy dates back to 5050 BC.

The Chinchorro developed three different styles of mummy—red, black, and mud-covered. Each body received a mask, and its organs were removed and replaced by a mixture of plants, mud, and sticks.

GRAVE MATTERS

Even after the Chinchorro stopped mummifying their people, the dry climate in Chile helped preserve many more bodies naturally. The Chinchorro people were named after a beach in Arica, Chile, where mummies were found in the 1960s.

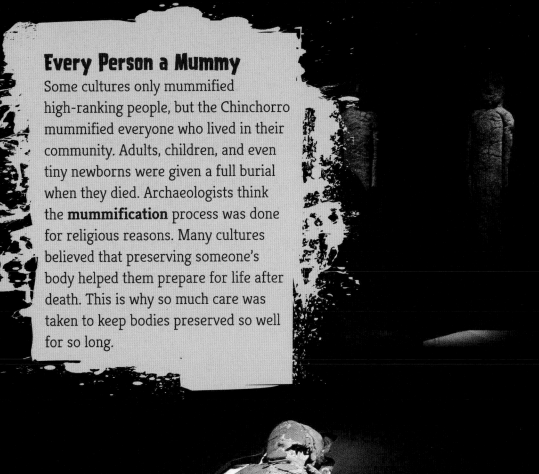

Every Person a Mummy

Some cultures only mummified high-ranking people, but the Chinchorro mummified everyone who lived in their community. Adults, children, and even tiny newborns were given a full burial when they died. Archaeologists think the **mummification** process was done for religious reasons. Many cultures believed that preserving someone's body helped them prepare for life after death. This is why so much care was taken to keep bodies preserved so well for so long.

Chinchorro mummies were created more than 2,000 years before Egyptians started creating mummies.

CRYPTS, TOMBS, AND OPEN AIR

Places with very dry air often cause bodies to mummify naturally. The mummies of Guanajuato (gwah-nah-HWAH-toh), a city in Mexico, were naturally mummified by the dry climate there. This also happens in cool, dry places such as crypts or tombs, where many cultures buried their dead. Krakow Crypt, part of a monastery in Krakow, Poland, has more than 1,000 naturally mummified bodies on the crypt's floor. Only their legs were covered in sand, while the rest of the body lay out in the open.

Dug Up Mummies

The 111 mummies scientists found in Guanajuato were actually bodies that were dug up between 1865 and 1958. A law said that families of buried people had to pay a tax to keep their bodies in the ground. Those who either couldn't afford or refused to pay the tax had their ancestors disinterred, or dug up, and placed in a building aboveground. Some of the bodies, including two very small babies, were actually embalmed by people before burial.

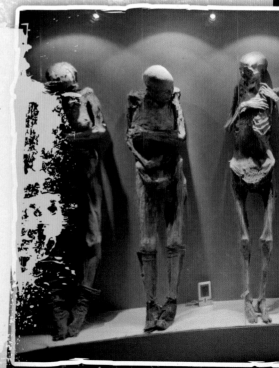

Some of the strangest naturally preserved mummies are in Tibet, China. The mummies, who died more than 4,000 years ago, were buried in upside-down boats in the Tarim Basin. The desert air prevented decomposition. Scientists discovered the mummies were actually of eastern European descent.

Krakow Crypt

GRAVE MATTERS

One of the Guanajuato mummies was only 24 weeks old when it died.

Scientists don't know why some Guanajuato mummies were embalmed because the climate would have naturally mummified the bodies.

MYSTERIOUS EMBALMING

We don't know how some ancient people preserved their dead. Some of the most well-preserved bodies have been discovered in China. In 1973, archaeologists began excavating a site in Changsha, China, where the Western Han dynasty buried their dead. Inside, they found the best-preserved mummy ever found. Xin Zhui, also called Lady Dai, is more than 2,100 years old and still has blood in her veins! Her body was completely intact, including her hair, skin, and even internal organs like her brain.

Scientists don't know how Lady Dai was preserved. No known embalming solutions were found in her body, but a clear liquid was in the bottom of her coffin when she was discovered. Archaeologists who first found her reportedly had skin rashes on their hands for months afterwards.

China's Sleeping Beauty

Xin Zhui's body was found inside the smallest of four nested coffins. Because her body was so well preserved, scientists were able to perform an **autopsy** on her. They discovered that she was overweight, had lower back pain, and her heart had clogged arteries! The tissues in her body were still soft, and her muscles even let her limbs bend. Scientists even know Xin Zhui's blood type! She was type A. She died between 178 BC and 145 BC, around age 50.

Xin Zhui was buried with more than 3,000
objects, indicating she was very wealthy.

GRAVE MATTERS

Because of her wealth
and amazing condition,
people call Xin Zhui the
"Diva Mummy."

EGYPTIAN MUMMIES

The most famous embalmed bodies were discovered by archaeologists in the pyramids and tombs of ancient Egypt. For more than 2,000 years, Egyptians prepared their dead through an elaborate mummification process. Egyptian kings, called pharaohs, built giant stone pyramids to hold their bodies after they died.

Special priests carried out the mummification. They took out organs and removed all moisture from the body with a salt called natron. After 70 days of prayer and preparation, the body was wrapped in bandages and put in a special coffin called a **sarcophagus**.

Mummification was a religious tradition for the Egyptians. They thought pharaohs were gods on Earth and needed to use their bodies after death. The body kept a person's soul and, without it, the soul could be lost forever.

Egyptians began making mummies about 2600 BC and continued for about 2,800 years.

Pull brain out through nose using a long hook.

Make cut on the left side of the body near the stomach.

Remove all internal organs.

Let internal organs dry out.

Put lungs, intestines, stomach, and liver inside jars.

Put heart back inside the body.

Rinse inside of body with wine and spices.

Cover body with natron for 70 days.

After 40 days, stuff body with linen or sand to give it a more lifelike shape.

After 70 days, wrap body from head to toe in bandages.

Place in coffin.

GRAVE MATTERS

The jars Egyptians used to store a mummy's organs were called canopic jars. They often looked like Egyptian gods.

Many of the Egyptian pyramids were built to honor Egyptian pharaohs, and they've lasted a long time. Some Egyptian mummies have lasted just as long! Many mummies have become very famous and helped us learn more about their fascinating lives.

Ramesses the Great (1303 BC–1213 BC) was one of the most powerful Egyptian pharaohs. The average lifespan for Egyptians at the time was 40, but Ramesses was over 90 when he died. He built more temples, monuments, and cities than any other pharaoh, and had more than 100 children. His body was moved many times because of **looters**, but it was discovered in 1881. It's one of the best-preserved Egyptian mummies archaeologists have found. Scientists have studied Ramesses's body and discovered battle wounds and health problems he developed later in life.

King Tut

Tutankhamun was an Egyptian who became pharaoh when he was just 9 years old. He ruled until his death at age 19. Tut's tomb was discovered almost completely untouched in 1922 by archaeologist Howard Carter. Tut's burial chamber had drawings and items in it that have helped scientists learn a lot about the ruler and how Egyptians lived during the empire's 18th dynasty, or around 1300 BC. Items from Tut's tomb, called artifacts, have toured around the world.

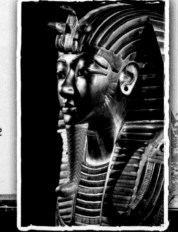

Some wealthy or important Egyptians

Temple of Queen Hapshepsut, a female pharaoh

GRAVE MATTERS

Even some animals were mummified by the Egyptians. Cats were considered sacred, and many were mummified and buried with their pharaoh owners.

19

NECESSARY DEVELOPMENT

One reason preservation techniques developed in some cultures is because of the wide travel many people began to undertake. During the Crusades, which took place between 1095 and 1291, European Christians were far from home when they died while fighting the Islamic Empire in the Holy Lands. Important noblemen were cut up, had their organs removed, and their bones boiled so they could be returned home for burial.

In 1300, Pope Boniface VIII issued a papal bull, or statement, which said that Christians could no longer cut up bodies for burial. Crusaders needed to find another way to preserve their dead for a proper burial. Europeans started to develop embalming methods to prevent the spread of disease and limit the smells of a decaying body.

Sicilian Mummies

People living on the Italian island of Sicily mummified their dead as well. The mummies were made by Capuchin friars who wanted to help people obtain blessed afterlives. The oldest known Sicilian mummy dates back to 1599. Most of the Sicilian mummies were drained of fluids, stuffed with straw or bay leaves, and kept in a vented chamber to let in air. Later they were washed with vinegar and either put in a coffin or hung on a wall.

Sicilian mummies

GRAVE MATTERS

Many mummies of Catholic saints are buried under the altars of churches in Sicily.

SELF-MUMMIFICATION

Some of the most fascinating mummies ever discovered are in Japan. In 2010, the well-preserved bodies of 24 Buddhist monks were found in the Yamagata region. There were stories of Buddhist monks who slowly mummified themselves, but none had been found until then. The monks did this to reach a final blessed state where there was no desire or suffering.

The monks, who lived in the early 1800s, spent a year eating nothing but nuts and seeds to remove all fat from their body. Next, the monks spent 1,000 days eating only bark roots and drinking poisonous tea. They stayed in stone tombs with a tube to help them breathe. They rang a bell each day to tell people on the outside they were alive. When the bell didn't ring, the tube was removed.

Final Wishes

One Russian Buddhist monk's final wish was that he be buried the way he died. Dashi-Dorzho Itigilov died in the lotus position, with his legs crossed, during a chant in 1927. The monk was buried sitting upright wearing the same robes he died in. According to his own wishes, Itigilov's body was dug up after about 30 years and was found well preserved. The body was dug up again in 1973 and found the same way. Itigilov is now on display in a Buddhist shrine in Russia.

This well-preserved Buddhist monk, who died during the 15th century, was found in India in 1975.

GRAVE MATTERS

The monks' bodies became poisonous to any animal that would have helped the body decompose after death. This includes maggots, which are the larvae of flies.

23

THE UNDERTAKERS

In the 18th century, Scottish scientist William Hunter was the first European to document draining blood and removing organs from a body to prevent it from decomposing. Called arterial embalming, it's the basis of all today's embalming methods. Modern preservation methods continued to develop in the late 1800s with chemicals like formaldehyde (fohr-MAL-duh-hyd). Bodies were also cleaned, which killed bacteria and prevented the spread of diseases like typhoid.

Before embalming, the most popular method of preserving a dead body during transportation or viewing was to pack it in ice or lay it on a table, called a cooling board, while an ice-filled box was put over the torso and head. With chemicals and the work of an **undertaker**, religious services and ceremonies could be performed with a much more natural-looking body.

William Hunter

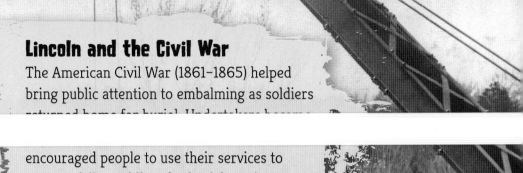

Lincoln and the Civil War

The American Civil War (1861–1865) helped bring public attention to embalming as soldiers

encouraged people to use their services to prepare fallen soldiers for burial services. Lincoln himself was embalmed and prepared for burial by an undertaker after he was **assassinated** in Washington, DC, in 1865. America's 16th president's body was viewed by thousands of mourners during its 13-day, 1,654-mile (2,662 km) journey home.

A crowd gathered to pay respects when Lincoln's body was dug up and moved in 1901.

GRAVE MATTERS

Lincoln's body was dug up multiple times to prevent it from being stolen. Years later, it still had many of Lincoln's facial features.

MODERN METHODS

We don't make mummies out of our dead these days. While bandages are saved for the living, bodies are taken through a set of steps very similar to those Egyptian priests used thousands of years ago. Today, modern undertakers work at funeral homes to help prepare bodies for burial.

Bodies are cleaned, and blood and other fluids are removed using a long needle, called a trocar. The blood in veins and organs is replaced by a solution, usually based on formaldehyde. The bodies are shaved, given pleasant expressions, and clothed in nice outfits. Last, undertakers apply special makeup.

Most modern embalming done today is meant to keep the body preserved for only a week or so. That's enough time to hold a funeral and give the deceased a proper burial.

Lenin's Tomb

Vladimir Lenin, who led the **communist** revolution in the Soviet Union, died in 1924. His body was preserved in the Soviet Union and has remained on display for nearly 100 years in Moscow, Russia. Lenin's body is kept at 61°F (16°C) and is routinely bleached and soaked in chemicals like glycerol and potassium acetate to keep mold away. Even Lenin's clothes are routinely changed. His embalmers claim Lenin looks better now than he did when he was alive!

Funeral homes do most embalming services for people.

GRAVE MATTERS

Most bodies in the United States and Canada are embalmed, but in most cases it's not required by law.

THE NEED TO PRESERVE

Humans have preserved their dead for thousands of years. Whether for religious reasons or as a sign of respect, our ancestors learned how to keep the dead from disappearing from sight. The desire to live forever still drives humans to develop new methods of preservation.

Some modern people have their bodies frozen by scientists after they die. In a process called **cryogenics**, scientists freeze dead bodies in solutions like liquid nitrogen, keeping them in temperatures as cold as −130°F (−90°C). People believe that scientists will one day be able to bring cryogenically preserved people back to life. Some have entire bodies frozen, while others freeze their DNA and hope to someday be **cloned**.

Perhaps one day, the preservation methods our ancestors developed centuries ago can be put to good use. Maybe our ability to preserve bodies will allow people to live far into the future!

GRAVE MATTERS

Walt Disney was rumored to be cryogenically preserved, but that's a myth. He was cremated when he died in 1966.

Frozen Baseball Star

The most famous person to be cryogenically preserved is baseball player Ted Williams. One of the best baseball players of all time, Williams was 2002. Williams' head and body are stored separately in the Alcor Life Extension Foundation facility in Arizona. Since his death, his head has been shaved and drilled with holes to keep it from cracking, although people have reported cracks have formed in the years since his death.

No one knows what will happen to cryogenically preserved bodies if the technology to bring someone back to life is never developed.

GLOSSARY

assassinate: to kill an important person in a surprise attack

autopsy: to examine a dead body to determine the cause of death

clone: to have an identical copy made using genetic information from the original

communist: someone who practices communism, which is a government system in which the government controls what is used to make and transport products, and there is no privately owned property

cryogenics: dealing with the freezing of dead bodies in order to preserve them so they can be brought back to life in the future

decompose: to decay

embalm: to treat a dead body with special chemicals to preserve it from decay

environment: the conditions that surround a living thing and affect the way it lives

looter: someone who steals from a place after it has been damaged by war, disaster, or time

mummification: the process of making a mummy

mummify: to embalm or treat a body in a way that preserves it for a long time

ritual: a religious or solemn ceremony consisting of a series of actions performed according to tradition

sarcophagus: a stone coffin

sphagnum: a moss that becomes compacted with other plants to form peat

undertaker: a person whose business is to prepare the dead for burial

FOR MORE INFORMATION

Books

Griffey, Harriet. *Secrets of the Mummies*. New York, NY: DK Publishing, 2013.

Pipe, Jim. *Egyptian Mummies: A Very Peculiar History*. Brighton, Great Britain: Book House, 2014.

Wilcox, Charlotte. *Bog Mummies: Preserved in Peat*. Mankato, MN: Capstone High-Interest Books, 2003.

Websites

Egyptian Mummies
si.edu/Encyclopedia_SI/nmnh/mummies.htm
Learn more about Egyptian mummies at this Smithsonian Institute website.

Mummies: Preserving the Dead
en.kids.da-vinci-learning.com/node/8325
Make your own real-life mummy with apples with this experiment.

Mummy Maker
kids.discovery.com/games/just-for-fun/mummy-maker
Learn how to make your own mummy with this great site.

Publisher's note to educators and parents: Our editors have carefully reviewed these websites to ensure that they are suitable for students. Many websites change frequently, however, and we cannot guarantee that a site's future contents will continue to meet our high standards of quality and educational value. Be advised that students should be closely supervised whenever they access the Internet.

INDEX